KILLER CATS

BOBCATS

By Ann Grucella

Gareth Stevens
Publishing

Please visit our website, www.garethstevens.com. For a free color catalog of all our high-quality books, call toll free 1-800-542-2595 or fax 1-877-542-2596.

Library of Congress Cataloging-in-Publication Data

Grucella, Ann.
Bobcats / Ann Grucella.
     p. cm. — (Killer cats)
Includes index.
ISBN 978-1-4339-6996-6 (pbk.)
ISBN 978-1-4339-6997-3 (6-pack)
ISBN 978-1-4339-6995-9 (library binding)
1. Bobcat—Juvenile literature. I. Title.
QL737.C23G78 2012
599.75'36—dc23

                              2011043594

First Edition

Published in 2013 by
Gareth Stevens Publishing
111 East 14th Street, Suite 349
New York, NY 10003

Designer: Daniel Hosek
Editor: Therese Shea

Photo credits: Cover, p. 1 Masterfile.com; all backgrounds, pp. 5, 6-7, 15, 21 Shutterstock.com; pp. 8-9 Tier Und Naturfotografie J & C Sohns/Workbook Stock/Getty Images; p. 11 Dr. Maurice G. Hornocker/National Geographic/Getty Images; p. 13 Michael S. Quinton/National Geographic/Getty Images; p. 17 Barbara Jordan/Photographer's Choice/Getty Images; p. 19 Altrendo Nature/Stockbyte/Thinkstock.com.

Printed in the United States of America

Contents

Boldface words appear in the glossary.

Danger in the Dark

The hungry animal waits in a tree for its **prey**. Though night has fallen, its eyes glow. Its brown fur and dark stripes make it nearly impossible to spot in the shadows of the forest.

Suddenly, it lifts its head. It hears something. An animal moves through the leaves below. Soon, the hunter spots its prey. The furry beast leaps from a branch and lands on a rabbit on the ground. It's time for the bobcat's dinner!

THAT'S WILD!

Bobcats have eyes that **reflect** light so they can see well in the dark. The light that seems to come from cats' eyes is called eyeshine.

Bobcats are sometimes called wildcats.

Big Cats

Bobcats look much like the cat you or a friend might have at home, but they're bigger. Some grow as long as 41 inches (104 cm). Their short, soft fur is often brown with dark stripes or spots. They have white fur on their belly.

Bobcats got their name from their short tail. A "bob" is another name for a short haircut. A bobcat's tail looks like it's been bobbed, or cut short. However, it's born with its bobbed tail.

THAT'S WILD!

Bobcats are about twice as large as house cats.

The tip of a bobcat's tail is black.

Built to Hunt

Bobcats are born to hunt. They have long legs and large paws. They don't often chase after prey. They hide, wait quietly, and then **pounce** when prey walks by. Bobcats can jump as far as 10 feet (3 m)!

Bobcats have deadly teeth. If you look in a house cat's mouth, you can get an idea of what a bobcat's teeth are like. The four longest teeth, called canines, are used to kill their prey. Other teeth are used for chewing and crunching.

Bobcats often eat a whole animal.

9

They're Everywhere

Bobcats live all over North America. They live in forests, swamps, and deserts. They may live on mountains and near towns. They like places with lots of plants and trees. These areas have many animals, so bobcats find it easy to hunt there.

There may be as many as 1 million bobcats between southern Canada and northern Mexico. However, bobcats are hard to spot. They like to move around at night and are scared of people.

THAT'S WILD!

There are more bobcats in North America than any other kind of big cat.

Bobcats' ears have a black tip. The back of each ear has a white spot.

What Bobcats Eat

Though bobcats mostly hunt at night, it seems like they're always moving. They only rest for 2 or 3 hours at a time. This means they need to eat—a lot!

Bobcats are **carnivores**. They eat many kinds of small animals, including bugs, fish, birds, rabbits, mice, and squirrels. Bobcats can also kill prey much larger than themselves. Northern bobcats can live on deer meat for several days. This is important during the cold winter months, when there are fewer animals to hunt.

This bobcat has caught a bird.

13

All Alone

With so many bobcats in North America, you might think they'd live in groups. However, female bobcats never share **territory**. Male bobcats may share some of their land, but they like to be alone, too. To let others know territory is "taken," bobcats leave their **scent** on plants, trees, and rocks. They scratch trees, too.

In **mating** season, a male makes his territory larger to find a female. When a female has babies, her territory becomes smaller because she doesn't like to go far from them.

By keeping other bobcats away, the big cats don't have to share food.

THAT'S WILD!

When a bobcat smells a scent, it may open its mouth. An **organ** in its mouth helps it figure out what the scent is.

Bobcat Homes

Because a bobcat's territory can be large, a bobcat often has more than one den. A cave or log makes a good main home. Bobcats may have other dens in parts of their territory they visit less often. These dens may be **brush** piles or rock overhangs.

Female bobcats often have dens that are very hard for other animals to find. This is because they need to keep their babies safe. Though few animals hunt adult bobcats, some—such as coyotes—eat bobcat kittens.

A male bobcat's territory is much larger than a female's.

Bobcat Babies

Male and female bobcats often mate in winter. About 2 months later, bobcat mothers—called dams—have one to six babies. The bobcat kittens are born with fur, though their eyes are closed. Their eyes open after about 10 days.

Bobcat kittens drink their dam's milk for about 2 months. Then, she brings them meat. Finally, she teaches them how to hunt for their own food. The kittens stay with their mother for up to a year.

THAT'S WILD!

After a year, a dam either makes her kittens leave or she leaves them.

These bobcat kittens are already good climbers.

Hunter and Hunted

For many years, bobcats were hunted for their fur. Many were killed by farmers **protecting** livestock. By the mid-1900s, there were few bobcats left in some parts of the United States. Laws were passed to protect them, and their numbers grew again.

Today, homes and roads built across bobcat territory cause more problems for the big cats. Besides losing dens, less land means fewer animals to eat. Bobcat territory may have to be protected in the future so they're around for years to come.

losing
homes to
building

losing
prey to
building

BOBCAT
DANGERS

hunted
for fur

killed by
farmers

Glossary

brush: cut or broken branches

carnivore: an animal that eats other animals

mating: coming together to make babies

organ: a body part with a special job

pounce: to jump suddenly toward or onto something

prey: an animal that is hunted by other animals for food

protect: to guard

reflect: to throw back light, heat, or sound

scent: a smell

territory: an area of land that an animal lives in and guards

For More Information

BOOKS

Marks, Jennifer. *Bobcats*. Mankato, MN: Capstone Press, 2011.

Squire, Ann. *Bobcats*. New York, NY: Children's Press, 2005.

WEBSITES

Bobcat

animals.nationalgeographic.com/animals/mammals/bobcat/
Hear what bobcats sound like.

Bobcat

www.defenders.org/wildlife_and_habitat/wildlife/bobcat.php
Read more about bobcats and the work being done to keep them safe.

Index